T0312893

SESSIONS 1 – 62

Sessions 1-62

Eli Goldblatt

Chax Press ◆ Tucson 1991

Session 5 appeared in Crankcase #1, and *Session* 45 in *Another Chicago Magazine* #16. *Sessions 1-33* was published as a handmade, limited edition book by Chax Press in 1988.

This publication has been made possible in part through the generous support of the National Endowment for the Arts, the Tucson/Pima Arts Council, Bookman's Used Books, and the Chax Press Members.

Chax Press is located in the historic Steinfeld Warehouse at 101 W. Sixth Street, no. 4, Tucson, Arizona 85701, USA.

ISBN 0-925904-06-6

Library of Congress Cataloging-in-Publication Data
Goldblatt, Eli.
    Sessions / Eli Goldblatt.
        p.   cm.
    ISBN 0-925904-06-6 (pbk.) : $9.00
    PS3557.03585S47   1991
    811'.54—dc20   90–15048
                                                              CIP

Sessions 1–33

for my father

Harry Goldblatt (1923-65)
doctor and lieutenant colonel

1

Witness recent events.
Must you react witlessly,
stupid against the blast?
How you fold your hands
as the news comes in,
how you wrinkle your coat.

You welcomed fire into your home

Open the door, window blinds up!
Cars in procession roll by.
Immoderate tho it may be,
I suggest at least
you weep at the graveside.

A simple change of place & occupation
requires the sun to stamp the pass.
The Highway knows the Notary seal
embossed in gold leaf, were
the traveller undocumented he
couldn't shift, she couldn't
practice any craft. The watch
is posted tho the road
seems clear. No one walks freely,
or gathers phlox unnoticed.

The boy remembered death,
the traffic circle, sycamores,
the corduroy pants he wore
by the lake. The boy expected
to die soon himself. No
angel appeared along the roadside
winter & spring he thought
he tried not to forget.
Maple leaf buds in a single
season,
  that is how they are
he felt the mind's delight
in words.

4

Tribes unsuited for industry
die organized battalions.
In a private education
each child grows to take
a lover, each child grows
to ride a steed.

Mother, your words were
meant for my ears.
A pond can't speak in
the voices humans hear there.

No roads go
between here & the colonel,
only stink lingers, a lewd
mantra & the semi-
automatic on the mantlepiece.
The cups empty refilled.
Markets sell goods the aged
can buy with coins.
I saw you reflected in store
windows, your black hair loose,
your arms bare. No prayer
goes from a city to heaven.
Backhoes dig pipe from the asphalt.
Wrap me in your yellow cloth,
love, can't you shield me
from my military sinew?

By what mentor can you save yourself?
The mill grinds wheat.
You mix flour, powder, water
knead the dough
let it rise, bake bread.
Set cloth on table
a wicker basket, knives, butter.
Uninvited guests arrive
the yearned for dinner unfolds
before you like a winter lake.
Garlic, pepper, basil, salt.
Taste consoles as it proclaims
pepper, garlic, salt, basil.
Finished, you want to nap?

Awaken, little minnow, time to gossip
time to carry on our pilgrimage.

Sand beside sea, sea
beneath sky
hand shading eye
the path thru mountains
body beside the grave

Please, dear woman, straddle
me, I'll press my face
to your breasts, even
our final shudder won't
disturb the embrace

Plum, plum seed.
One man, two men, a dozen.
One woman, two women, a dozen.
No wrinkle in the cloth we put on
nor wrinkle in cloth put off.
Armies fall on their swords
& we with them.
Private garden walls
each neighbor at leisure
speaks against neighbors
weapons gathered by dozens.
Plum flower orchards
burned to stumps.

Threads ring the moon
body, the dead
honey in sun's heat.
Each child born reflects
light, the threads
lead house to house.
Play on lawns, swim
the lake, stretch.

Mortar set brick
holds back armies
a time. Soldiers
reflect light,
that is how
we see them.

Don't purse your lips
Earth slopes moss & bracken
Breathe in, Breathe out
Take off your gear! make
way for shake
Wood can't sluice the flood
nor fiber staunch Time's blood
Camera relax your grip
the picture's a verb hurled
against cinder, cedar cone
roots, maple flowers to seed
What fool do you know
who won't go? None.
We're all called.

(to paradise)

Bom ta ra
Bom ta ra
We march patched
 & pandied
Bom Bom tow ta

Swarm petals, scatter bees
Lift the crowd from their knees
Ta ra Ta tay

O sober up the watch sergeant
Awaken the sisters asleep
scratch a match, scratch a match
Too Toom
  loo rag
Bottles roll
  polished halls
Wallowers smooch
please please please

Taka dan Taka dak
Parade ground weeds

With our packs on our backs
we waved to our in-laws
away to the forest
where wild teachers taught us

Ta low Ta lawk

There's a heavenly ladder
There's a hell bent balloon

Bou tow doon
Bou ta doon

Open, villian, let the door swing!
red meat, corn, fish
squashes, apples, rice
larder's full up
rats fatten in the cellar.

Open, poet, let the poem
wobble out of doors. You
of all jailers know to cut
thongs & crossbars.

Open, poem, no
air about the flame
snuffs embers out.

(Sweet

                colophon
embark again for print
from your
flat above a pet store
You're a

newspaper disguised
vellum altar when
letters press blind
militant

O yes what you say

has texture, arouses
the twill
hipbones tipped up
for a plunge
Murder mirrors—
hasty, too—tho

windows gather shine
Look Out

you most of all)

For rickets drink
myrtle wine.
Shade, sit
beneath wheat heads.

I would feed children stone.

Casseroles in the kiln
glaze turn glass
heat a means
to make a dish

Eat it from my hand

Bee bop do wee
No disease I don't command
Scoo dop doo
from my stove to you

(the will to reflect)

Terrace a sill to the dark lake
merry among the skillful dancers
No ditties they don't find steps for
no entreaties they can't bargain
into profit

Cage together two tree shrews, baboon
pheasant, ground squirrel, albino crow
rooster in red tinsel
penguin gliding under water

Settle around a window looking out
Did you remember to bring tobacco?

So much death
settles in her mind
cancer easily seizes the blood
mother & a child boating drown
as she spins wool

Cloak enough to break
autumn breeze. A fire
warms the hands, rain
tamps the mounds

Let shuttle sing between
flax strands, let weft
face the beater buries
line by line rise up
a fabric worn
in winter

You could be wrong about sense
what the judge wants upon the bench
storm lifted off
lyrics performed by choir

Here among the stoops & posts
one of us couldn't work
she sat & fitly sang
refused tunes
fashioned from newsprint

Ta rull taka da
The angels here grow old while I
weary of civil mystery
Crack lungs Kaa Taa sing
instead of pray or pesticide
Bikee Boot pina poot
serve up spittle, let fly
bile among the marigolds
Hur Ker ma ruc
love flesh whose surface
scars, heaven or no
so far to go till irises
arise lee mee thru
winter loam frost Ghost!
Lakes contain the fish
clouds swim past quick
insects   mook
Embrace ice you fire

(harlequin)

                mind covered in
red blue-green patches
upon which rock the I stands
draws forward in this jazz.
Tatters unravel & fall from

a beggar comic soldier who can
tell jokes for real covered
as he is by mortar fire.
"Music, hon, that
I can't stand—you
want me to cry?" Go

ahead, turn off
                    the radio.
Let's sit in the dark
& see what they find so funny.

(amalgalm)

twenty below sun melt
tar roof! when
               mercury
spreads over gold
             the precious
dissolves in the quick

Be wise
fish
   belly up in algal bloom

**

All my sudden belongs here
ain't no ninny 'neath a tree

how without hurting another
soul an easy excuse
for marching
            orders
taken from the top

**

Be cold says the sun
   a frightened dog bites
He knows his time
   but not his way home

**

whose horserace on whose
horse?
      singing
          when soul's
not the center
        a sham
copernican revolution

Men marching
     set to shoot
        soft metal
Death ring
      unsanctified by dog
or fish

**

a buddha
       bundle the leaves shade
not embroidered,
             a woven sack

No eloquent
order from the top down
the sun
     belly up

Beneath this roof
we eat food
        got by theft

wallet sized cellophane
Is that what you call your flesh?
or caught in a potato
dirt side named skin

a flash will kick you
Helmeted, creaking from too Great a Weight
into the end zone

encapsulate, who
can withdraw a self, self-
potter shaping the clay but
notice the wallet sized clefts in pores of the hand
poost taka painful fissures
nothing fills silence like a soup 'o
red vegetable matter
a picture to slip between diaphanous sheets

god mercury held within the tube
tells temperature shapes itself to its marked cylinder

You wonder flowing
what's left to flow once
your fluid leaks away
That way he plays the game helmeted.

(harpy muse evoked)

so much flesh
gathered in your hands
not any one sex,
mind you,
              or ellipse
perfected upon foci—
early
        matter making up
bird's wing or currish
behavior on the part of human
pigment,
              the off-oval it assumes
on canvas.
              Bury me
bury my poem if you will
but don't forget our arrangement,
reader,
          your mufti flatters
roving me
              to prayer
that we'll not leave
each other either on the ground
or in the air.

Weee er lie eea
The skalding hand
lipket   sollke do
praise in praise who
Ker mur solly
        tinkmi spee
I looked into your eyes
    one eye at a time limlimlimk
could you be

Critik eye
     to whisper love subterfuge
winking paper baubles
I propose   surrender
take off the uniform
resign your commission
step down from chair & tables

who among us raises the least cry

whittle a memory
The seven pathways lead no where
a child is born or dies
Whittle the gunstock into a winding sheet

     step down

let the hurricane wet your stockinged feet

spirit pinches cheeks a ripe
    plum bitten to the stone
no more good will come of it
        than ill
make a meal, bake a pie
sew a bird's head to your epaulet

you want to Make Sense join the army

a weasel in among canary daffodils
   whispers
      "Mar kertel
a melody to measure right from wrong
  seepes   seepes   seepex
a ladder to heaven
    & memory to bar the gate
        ruliuckee o little
teeth catch your vermin
    quick   quick

Later or tomorrow perhaps
I'd like to confer with my father
clear up the confusion

Tho he died on a bed
not a pure soldier
                    in war

The spider already
at the corner of my eye
speaks
neither by trick
                    nor omen
to the end of the sentence.
You would hardly recognize me
I belong so much to this world.
Sit down in one of two chairs,
spider, that we may spin.

The dead have no solution to wars.

In this nation-state among
built objects more valued
than desired we draw
our pay or not
                    A mercy
or a sore opens each account—
& adds—till children
challenge the tender   Death

pays cash, dad, you know
the musical where Ride-
a-pony makes millions
girl subsumed in the bargain

Wax we're made of,
daddy, sweating
while the wick burns

(dear dad / signed son)

Step aside Angel decanted from despair. Living lips refute you.
I want to look at my dead old man. No fort can hold his gaze
off, nor can brick speech hide me long. Syllables cast like sticks
not the missile lingam interposed between me & void. Ta ree
Ree Tay

The gaze & no designated god to put it right. Small boy brings
offerings, I write, epistle press on the curtain you there once
photographic Helmet above the squat smile. Cast sticks te tay
contain fire you not in among the icons. A session disappearing
after now

                                                    you see, father
brother, not a feat to last. You're distant from cries. Behind
you further fiction melts in heat we lend the sun. I write from
a material world. Therefore I often forget.

Wake up, little sister self, soldiers
disdain you as ghostly old
honeycomb   Plumtree remind
me this rain ree
ree is your rain

A jun-
gle for lungs
you find people
scorn your beard
little father
mist bespeaks mourning
Eyes the lakes
sailors tack upon

(innkeeper's companion)

I sit down at the door
each day
          my dog head
poised between bark & sleep

Ghosts mean nothing
                    I want to say
Leave the dooryard clear
for the troops to return

Yellow leaf falls at the year's last gust
     no battalion lanterns
               nor even a footfall
I bite at the curtain foot
bite my front paw sore

too little decorum, too
few paying guests

(discord da lu tay)

Hunger pulls the journeyer from the grave
where he laid in august
                           lapel ornaments
                    brass on hat
Overexposed
                  photo retains a face
In mirror, another

          Lift your wine, boys
Sing out your hebrew dirge to
sanctify the Lord
men & dead together
(this side the curtain
mourners sharpen prayer
for war

Mother in her frown can't smile
nor children permitted to mourn

Are you, son, a child?

(yom kippur curtain)

who
declares all vows & oaths void
for sin we committed in anger

     kindles festival lights
           across blessing

(a soldier's job
       doesn't belong in verse

Atone—
     to be struck
dumb—
      sin thru unseeing
harm done
       we soldiers
to an idea. A
         drape over the soldier's
box prevents,
        a curtain before the Holy
of Holies admits

                        Yizkor has begun
            to recall those
                        dead by camps flash seizure
                        buried or burnt

We less than grass blades
lean beside graves
                        the mind keeps
Tho weepers be ten thousand strong,

weep

33

for M.E.K.

I feel certain the man is dead
You wouldn't let me in to see him
even tho I can't go back

Two men cross a bridge
over a frozen stream
One left his family years ago
the other only some days gone

I feel a certain man died
You don't let me know who
nor can I go along to see

Water runs underneath ice
To fish swimming in pools
spring means nothing

A flood beneath my manners
I'm crouched on the ice
in a child's attitude:
I refuse to go home

1/23/85

A hundred hunkered

A hundred hunkered

Smiles, chills the manly man rides
thru the forest with bells on
A hundred hunkered because their
cause was no fiction   rocked
the chassis built to carry
troops home,
                    the story goes
(machine to pinch the Kaiser
separate peas into size categories

We resist 3 bells   latch
the back gate to prevent bricks
slipping out
                    Maybe
rumors don't fit her palm
maybe
she's not war or a goddess

Then a lot of us don't care about that.
You can't see what's
                         in other pay envelopes.

Violet incarnation
pressed fire to forehead
One brother met another
cancelled sense, our brawl
took hell to court
A peak to his felt hat
says more than gun could
about the weapons he chose

           fathers caught
in the branches of sycamores
lining the boulevard.   Huh!
you wouldn't break a sewer
What water to piss in

Be wealthy among sibs.

Suitors release a scent
dragonflies above marsh
We amass debt
           Surface repays
deep creatures its kiss, it's

manly solace:
           open more bottles
or the clay court play—there
we each sound our voices

Pincer welt

Pincer welt raised on her arm
a sign that diet
        applied from without
works within

Meters mark our autos

Light goes off under brew
Corinto's mined harbor
a bay in back pages

Alarums carry the boots
& badges you recognize designed
to emit peace
                after a busted chain

Hulls, hulls take off
the air mixed in his canteen
avails him a posture
                        Poised
to strike a sparrow

Make marrow your meat,
        hunters   Pursue
when game is near & home
at your back saying 'bye

The Inner Weave

Orange flask above lumber rows
peaked homes swoon in minus sun
or suffer muck

Shower for cleansing skin
so much to wash off   water
rushes us to towelling

You swallow weave.
Carpet at your feet   blue
country borders a more
ornate red   just so
we can reconcile
colony to master

Outside iron dust
still falls like whiskers.
Successful cars carry a message
over the broken snow.

Liquid cough lover
sitting the toilet & sneezing
water running away with us
A kiss, please, sweet

Whether
man & woman
have to be
or not
        water level
well up on the flood wall
left its mark

A shepherd doubled back
after his flock died in the jaws,
cleanest servant who
ever trod or was,
the mime wonders above earth
why they won't address him

Home akin to
accent to our speech

Buried oils release angels
I wander corn rows.
A survivor bears children of survivors
the camps her inflamed organs now.

Cloth rubs down your face
Skin allows only a little water to enter.

Begin to mark the forehead
these pages form,
white quiet cat
beside my notebook
keeps danger near,
that I not forget
sauntering among demon angels
rejoicing over drowned soldiers

widow remains widow
& orphan orphan
The blast would have us forget

Keep sullen counsel
here among fruit trees,
blanket to cover the shiver
in thighs. A dog

barks at birds raising song—
blast-rush as trains
roll past our station—
little we understand

still mind

A chain of deaths
or deaths in dream
bring me to my self
again to remember,
not only memory but to
recognize substance

one often forgets
A struggle between horizontal
& vertical
master & colony
for riches reside in the moment
but the linear means produce
Set politics reeling
reeling within, without

go fishing but catch what?
Our water comes from a lake
lake from streams, the streams
spring from earth on which rain falls.
Water pools to a proper depth for fish
& we fish with baited hooks.

Cape Cod Marconi Area

As well mention dunes
that wall the beach
or blue above the ridge brush

eyes don't hold much sand

as dream
a crocodile bound down
for a child's toy—

sand might be boulders
given the proper size

unbottled quaver belling
out above tidy doorways
to paradise purchase.

Flat beach rollers
smooth
       spicules
& shudder,

we love here.
Vetch roots
on dunes, monies

preserve a saltbox
house at the dune's edge.

What we want

Horoscopes that come true
form a quandary: why
I belong beneath a tree
cool in summer, aged
in fall, in spring new buds,
but winter finds me
casting sticks.

Haven't you approached the mark?
patience alone can't bring
you closer, nor moderation
carry you over
              solemn business;
take a pill to break its back.

Fate itself can't operate
where it's not observed.

Point of Rock Road

Sun made that shadow,
I know, the bush
flowered with petals outnumbering
leaves, half-shaded pinks
among grass stalks.

No need to conjure in love's name
nor grow wealthy by design

We saw the bush
I forgot until I saw
this picture.
We were there,
saw those flowers
in afternoon shadow.

We just walked
to the bay beach that time.

photograph of zede

hunger strike or, dirt
washed from his skin, tallis
laid like light about his limbs.
He reads a book.
Neither need to eat
nor cause to cut food off
enters here, reader,
where
      you sit—
won't you take a pear?

Count the days he's held the fast.
Neither sin nor policy
drains him like these hours do
death figures in a cloth edition

      The news arrives thru
      window or door:
      they have refused a claim
      dispensed a mercy
      or lifted no ban

Dream without food
what hunger have you,
                reader

So wet

High life get
you gone
   back to you home,
best said:
un-
  comfort let
      my bones know salt
weather watching.
Artful arcade
     construed
above us
    we walk thru
wary tho we be
can I see what
     you, mother, saw before you
or you, father, before you:
The Speeches?
     ringing us, a
sparkle atop the elephant cage—
trainer beware!   I swear
I saw a lion want to pounce
(for instance
scones hold raisins
   or roses
bred for show left home too soon)

          Desire
fired by lies
denial shakes this world:
numble
          rack a tap
                    solve-Ay-shun YAH
I requite my fillings not by cups
but seeming rain when weather comes
is rain to
          soak these bones
so wet

Harbor your inchings here
among books aches prosper
salamanders breathing in mud

A moment's rest in embroidered chair

you remember so much you want
to say about this world, stock

sayings or new, nor are you
helpless to mend a crushed

bone or darn socks, hand
round while guns allow

loaves that last. Roads
that carry goods all ways

deliver brows to gun butts,
command given to artists in flesh.

A sonnet says joy,

bullet gouge, set type waiting
for the ink roll. Reader,

approach along the gravel path—
children swim the pond, diving
from a float
             In daylight when
parked cars burn, sun renders
flame insubstance
while at night we see
the fires for miles set
round the city

silhouette can monster madness

On grid set sidewalks
I pass windows displaying bone
beg me buy a scoop
from the cut glass vat

Judith slew Holofernes
under such circumstance

or so we read.

I get up

from mire & fallen leaves
to climb the hill hip

stretch my arms past wicker sand baskets
more than my mind can give

neither city stone
nor village thatch
more mercy more mercy more
cunning washed into the streams

A smudge against our cheeks
rubbed on can as well rub off.

Your voice your muscle in my arm
urge me to carry the carcass
until no more flesh clings to the sentence

I raise my hands uselessly
raise my voice to an accustomed pitch

A clatter down hill to frozen
similar triangles
                    dim lake jetty out into past
cold rain turn gray twigs brown—

a political geography
you react you mesmerized

No
not enough in verbal triumph
Willing dupe must walk alone to do penance
put this burden down & pick up your arms

Nights grown colder inhere
a hundred grim for survival,

brown breast burst as well as a white dam
your platelets sealing the room

Stand back!

fire breaking a log jam water couldn't
you could almost notice me crouched among

I watched an unfurnished quality
creep among my things,
nouns modified by eastern light;

up along with steam in radiator pipes
the guilt the anger
warms the room as it comprehends me.

Tho law revert to give & take

Today the glass ark opened
& they paraded lungs not the Law
around the awe-struck chamber.
Bride of my Bride!
                    Constable of my Constable!
a bliss awaits those who serve
but we who burrow, we who
clear debris away cycle thru sow
& butcher, sit like tea in the cup.

Comfort, brick face wall
draw silver thorns around you
a peaceful
   talisman, offer relief
like sand receive your share
from the sea
   Bricks in the fire
can't move in their heat

But to say the thing itself?

In Guatemala early evening
   the army band would play
tourists, townfolk, peasants promenade
girls arm in arm
    boys arm in arm
marches & brassy dance tunes surrounding
no comfort at the heart

Over & above
   I want to reach
a thing
  there is—
    couldn't a person believe
smoke drifts across a red brick face
from where I sit

content you fill you up
                    let go
the ballast the barrack the benthamite
doctrine,
              knowing the way is to live
                                      Live
dawn chimney-smoke curls around itself
stop sign shadow squat on eastern wall
the light full wind orange surge
to day yellow
                what it holds
what it is
          content
shadow beside the office-goer
    blue shade just giving over
red wood fence into sun
No metaphor dissolves
                        the whole in its
liquid parts.

Child coming

Sessions 52–62 *for Wendy*

This is the Pesach—
not limbs so many
sticks for the woodpile to stoke
the oven that burns memory off
(only ash witness,
                  a mute soot)—
sacrifice said to redeem by memory
hard labor for nothing
as tho I had been there

Not a seamster
sewing scene by scene together
I hum again a dim tune
deem
     ree ree
         dom
blood spilt from the free cup
masterslaveslavemaster
murmured means nothing
a soot suit sown in fought furrows
I know I was there says the book
passed over   redeemed for a time
now can I only remember
dime into dollar into dime?

            Dealer, play a card
hard labor to remind a child
what his father lost
(no thing) & in the basement hanging wet
clothes what my mother said to me
ree dee dom you're a son
                here in spring
tree leaves bud again
over those withered in other weather

Memory is melody

intoxicant
                (a full house hand
can't buy a full house back),
I bottled spirit
hold my breath unleavened
"For what the Lord did for *me*"

yoga pose

How bunched they leave the womb
close to each other's surface
clinging clustering at the goat gate
minding each other's entering
& eat all at the doorstep crouched

Speech set at the next dupe's throat
a kiss like twined herbs over arbor arch
Go to your banquet, banker child
your cloister, monkish babe
shack, master poor boy
Iron jacks them apart
                    the stink
in small space where blue bus
takes away the injured famous
who groveled for puritan pennies.

*   *   *

Then burst your bright sings
sin urge star-solid
smoke bends as if in asana
final we breathe
                   unmilled matter—
muscle & syntax
be brave! Animal self
easily stunned easily bathed
in a sea fusion will warm

Sunny at ground zero

Fire worms round the block
across from Pennypack Park.
An ashen mulch covers the walk,
brick face smudged and toothy
timber stuck up where a wall was.
Go lie on the grass, Preston Howard,
remember your home in there among
burnt studs. Welcome the green
freedom dispossession brings, & join
the many flowers cultivated
by the Park Commission.

What I Voted For

So stark the poem grows
while sun don't shine
or I run beside the lake & watch
men cast their lures; one fat
fisher listens to the tunes,
his swivel desk chair set
on grass. All that stripped
away all so piled up—
                           in my dream
the child sees on a door a plaque
proclaiming my own death—
                              lake front
property owned by no realtor
or the State,
                a common lawn
you live on all your life.

Some caught, some let go
Speaker wires torn from their posts
& 2 channels lost of voice & music

It's what I voted for
what the postcard I got in the mail
announced:
          "Yes I have, yes"

But in this poem naked
I want your body beside mine sleeping
(& won't forget the child travelling
alive between 2 parents

Food fills the belly

I stop & start
                wishing for a child
when I saunter past these store displays.
All the time a hammer
strikes flat steel.
                The child cries;
we lost her but she remains between us.
A model apartment complex built
down the street beside late night music
bars, the newspapers report wars my people
fund & shame we have a hand in, among

these I declare my desire to raise a child.
I turn away from shouts because I say I can't do
much, but the child calls in a smaller voice—
the far-away war is in it, relief too

that a wanderer has come home, even the dead one
who returns in dream to delight his family.
No words, then only the announcer speaks
after the song fades out.
                        Food fills the paper sacks,
bottles the slim bags, but a hammer hits the limit
of its swing & air carries the steel shock. Radio

silence doesn't charm me; I want to hear
in this rich city. A prosperous citizen listens
less & less but that's me inside a brittle shell,
food for shore birds.

Is it a wheel or a path?
An owner of the park crept up
bent, barely seeing but belonging
to this circle of flowers, trees.
He & mates flowed around the walk
marking willow trunks; beetles
trundled sacred thru moist soil.
How helpless he had made himself
no onlooker could say. We saw
only arms & legs going to dust.

A mercury world with a mound angry to the touch
as sleep rubs your eyes. Neither cords nor
guy-wires secure this land, nor do grubs burrow
in flesh they remember wearing themselves.
You'd like it, you'd think it strange
when tunes catch ice in their beaks & fly.
A fish spark jaundices the holiday crowd;
the squirrel speaks haltingly among his peers,
tho across species his eloquence is infamous.

That day came, and with it my last chance both to say
good-bye & to tell him how angry he had made me.
How good I was—no way to get warmer or to battle
hunger & thirst—how I wished to

                              re-live previous taunts
in another body, another walk around the grounds.
You matter to me. The more I refuse silhouettes,
the harder it will be to leave without a choir or parcel

but I want to welcome you back to our balloon.

Nabaj, 1980

Walk back thru gods to a village
blue & pink walls, dirt streets
pine pitch smell after rain.
The storyteller's accent sharp at first
rounded into story after drink.
But nothing will pass thru that gate
even tho a 16 year old stands
in her great skirt crying because
they won't let her brother out.

The authorities came with bulldozers
& an army carrying picks as well as guns.
Above all, they have a world to build.

Story made only of memory & we need to find out
so much about the brain. Where does longing
come from, & the swift police action that follows?
Cruelty and mean spirit
                              were the benches upon which
men waited to be identified or perhaps inducted or shot.
Women gathered in the square outside the barrack
demanding to see their husbands & sons. After a time,
soldiers fired into the crowd on the square, killing twenty.

This is a poem, & the mind reaches to embrace kin
in a poem thru metaphor. A village is not an image
nor are women shot in a square
symbols for the waiting mind.

days after atonement

Yes I saw them standing
among crates & dynamos, a soft
crater each man's heart
                              each woman's hand
a reliquary
                Ballots & cummerbunds leaned
against the wall, by secret word they
told what body count could be
                Bursting
                              silver money
backed by calabash of street talk.

While we whiled the sunny afternoon away,
fleets set sail to treat the oil fields
righteously. All hearts joined hands
to hymn a biblical:

                Ladles stir the stew
           Lords exchange for futures due,
           & coiled like memory the serpentine
           poor wait 'round the thorn tree.

Suddenly Jump-up looked back & woke
the neighborhood at half past two:

>It's humans, captain, everywhere
>smiting & smitten beneath the power lines.
>Yellow ribbons flick among the brick debris.
>A little smoke, a smudge, & water fit
>to burn a beetle's holy carcass.

No sins among the lonely or the dead.

Miller grinds grain between stones, mitre
box guides the carpenter's saw to bevel
matched ends, I plant a shoot in new soil,
& singer joins memory & melody in song.

What notice will we receive for all we've done?

We see a destiny in our give & take. Rails
fit the wheel's groove because we cast them so,
& master expects courtesy from slave.

A square deal for the children

An edge we wander between circle & silver
becomes a pocked road. Skin wrinkles
& burn holds its place with scar. You motion,
I inch along behind, but no ledge leads home.
The pitch gets steeper. We climb or hold to a
moving belt that stretches above us straight
to the vault.

        I rush to wait.
The street my youth called home grew ice,
a sag remnant whittled from light.
All muscles strain for soldiers that
parade; we whistle as they march by.

    The raw bill came
as I sat beside the ramp.
Lights switched off.
The wounded died & the whole
resumed their tasks.

Tanks rolled across lawns. Men
pretended soldiers always grew
there by the chain link fence.
Machines furrowed the prized plots.

Child coming

But a child is coming into our home.
Better the monkeys & cockroaches parade by
& act up without rhyme or moral than soldiers
with a mission should enter a town held by rebels.

Actual men & women this poem can't grasp or conjure up
live far above traffic & others, wrapped in newsprint,
sleep on the street. I'm afraid for our new child
not because a poem can be fancy like a toucan or
that by prophesy Ezekiel brought life to dry bones.

No, the flesh we are told will wither
but in our minds we can even forget to live.
I want to be here among these words for you
& alongside you, too, tho that is given time

which for instance my father forfeited
by overwork & then lost in his death.
O yes, now I'm afraid for myself
as I have never had reason to be before.

All those guns & fiefdoms out there,
those mouthed words & a silver medal
laid out on a cotton nest in a flocked box.
I should say I'm ashamed for this world
I have not tried hard enough to change

        but I'm happy to think I will
hold you soon & eventually hear what you say
seeing the crowd at City Hall or corn stalks
drying after harvest. My work life, too,
will take me away from you. Better
the bedbugs should draw no conclusions
than sailors train big cannon on a city.

My poem itself adopted like you.

Eli Goldblatt was born in 1952 in Cleveland, Ohio, and grew up on Army posts in the U.S. and Germany. After college and odd jobs in farming, manufacture, and carpentry, as well as a year in medical school, he taught science and math for five years in an inner-city alternative high school in Philadelphia. He studied literature and composition at the University of Wisconsin-Madison, and is currently an assistant professor at Villanova University.

He has previously published two childrens' books (*Leo Loves Round* and *Lissa and the Moon's Sheep*, Harbinger House), one verse play (*Herakles*, Tamarask Press), and two books of poetry: *Journeyman's Song* (Coffeehouse Press), and *Sessions* (Chax Press, 1988; includes the first 33 sections of *Sessions 1-62*). He lives in Philadelphia with his wife, visual artist Wendy Osterweil, and their son Leo.